PEACE WALL

Scripture Art –
Inspirational verses
from the Bible

DAWNLIGHT
PUBLISHING

...And your feet shod
of the gospel of peace

I0559868

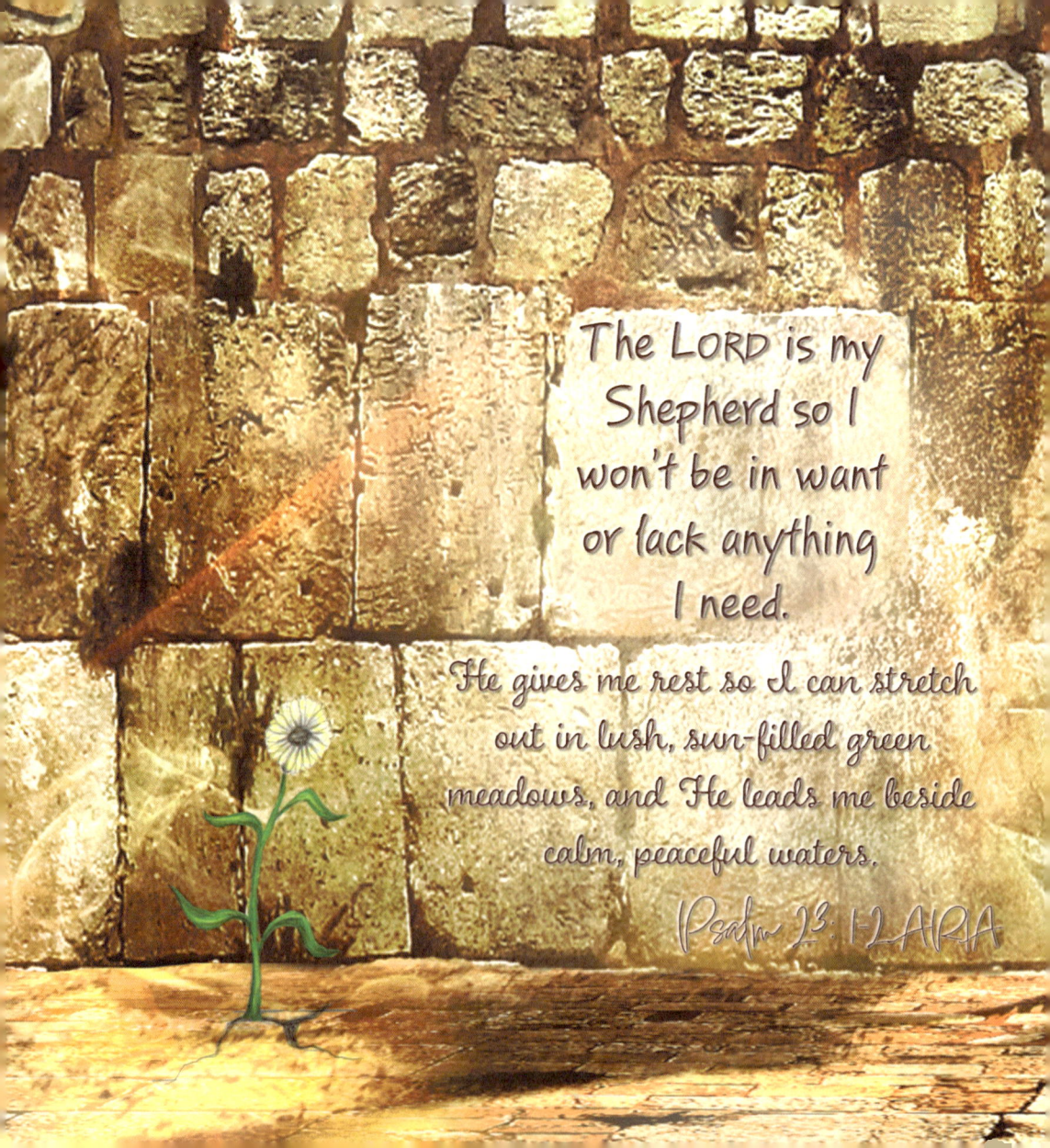

The LORD is my
Shepherd so I
won't be in want
or lack anything
I need.

He gives me rest so I can stretch
out in lush, sun-filled green
meadows, and He leads me beside
calm, peaceful waters.

Psalm 23: 1-2 AIA

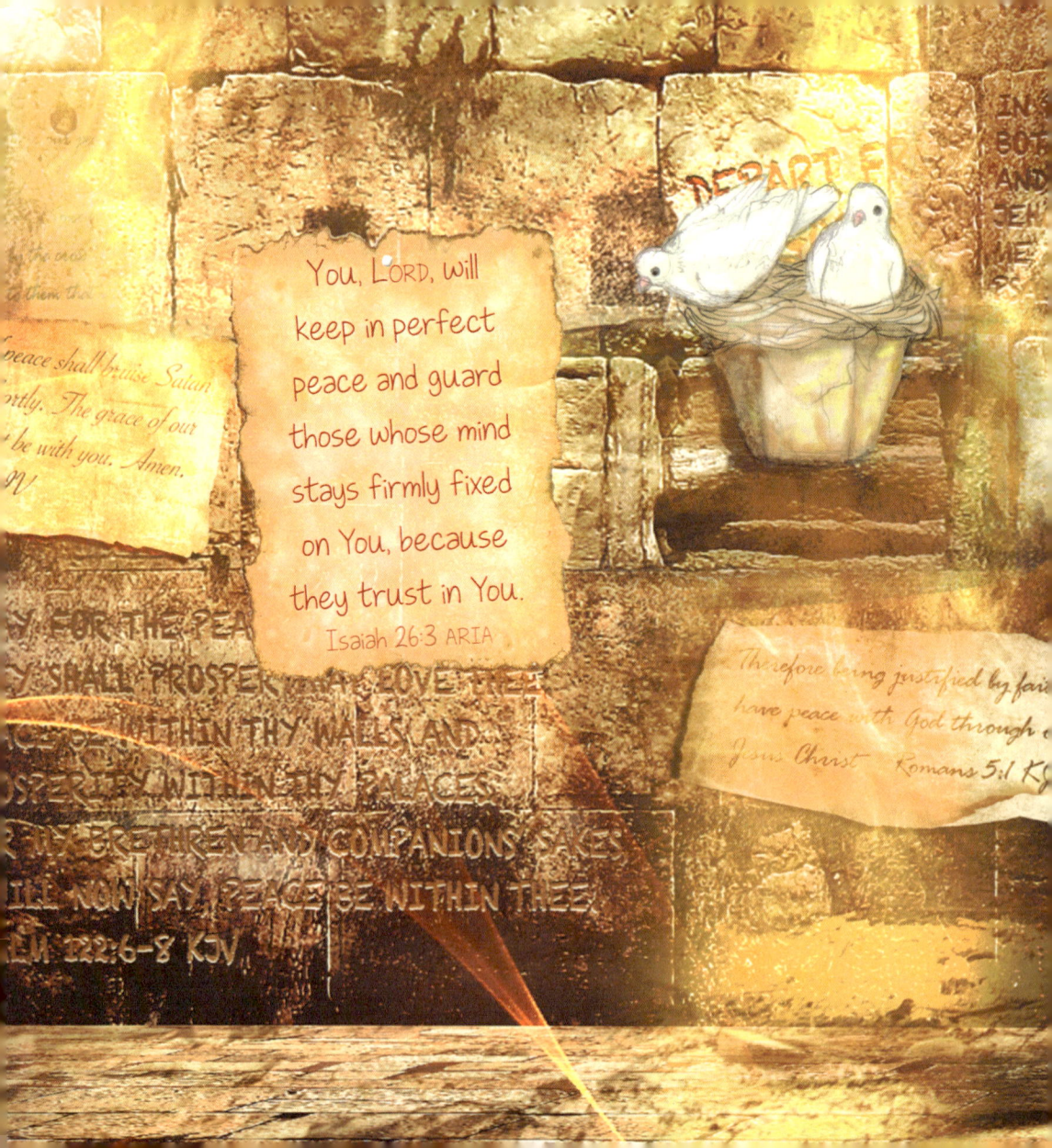

You, LORD, Will keep in perfect peace and guard those whose mind stays firmly fixed on You, because they trust in You.

Isaiah 26:3 ARIA

peace shall bruise Satan
ortly. The grace of our
be with you. Amen.
V.

Therefore being justified by fai
have peace with God through
Jesus Christ   Romans 5:1 KJ

FOR THE PEA
SHALL PROSPER LOVE THE
WITHIN THY WALLS AND
OSPERITY WITHIN THY PALACES
BRETHREN AND COMPANIONS SAKES
LL NOW SAY PEACE BE WITHIN THEE
EM 122:6-8 KJV

STAND THEREFORE, HAVING GIRDED YOUR LOINS WITH TRUTH, AND HAVING PUT ON THE BREASTPLATE OF RIGHTEOUSNESS, AND HAVING SHOD YOUR FEET WITH THE PREPARATION OF THE GOSPEL OF PEACE. Ephesians 6:14-15 ASV

In nothing be anxious; but in
everything by prayer and
supplication with thanksgiving
let your requests be made
known unto God. And the
peace of God, which passeth
all understanding, shall guard
your hearts and your thoughts
in Christ Jesus.

Philippians 4:6-7 ASV

"The mountains will leave their stations and the hills will disappear when they slip away; but My kindness will never leave you. Neither will My covenant of peace be removed," says the Lord who showers you with abundant mercy.

Isaiah 54:10 AKJA

Peace, peace to him
that is far off, and
to him that is near,
saith the LORD; and
I will heal him.

Isaiah 57:19b KJV

Therefore being justified by faith
have peace with God through ou
Jesus Christ   Romans 5:1 KJV

"I have spoken these things to you, so that in Me you will have peace. In the world there will be tribulation, but be cheerful as I am the One that is already victorious in this world." ~Jesus

JOHN 16:33 ARIA

The LORD shall
fight for you,
and ye shall
hold your peace.

Exodus 14:14 KJV

...eace shall bruise Satan
...rtly. The grace of our
...be with you. Amen.

Therefore being justified by faith
have peace with God through o
Jesus Christ   Romans 5:1 KJ

...Y FOR THE PEA...
...Y SHALL PROSPER...LOVE THEE
...WITHIN THY WALLS AND...
...PERITY WITHIN THY PALACES.
...HE BRETHREN AND COMPANIONS SAKES
...LL NOW SAY PEACE BE WITHIN THEE
...LM 122:6-8 KJV

The God of peace shall bruise Satan under your feet shortly. The grace of our Lord Jesus Christ be with you.

ROMANS 16:20 KJV

Her (wisdom) ways
are ways of
pleasantness, and all
her paths are peace.
Proverbs 3:17 KJV

The Lord bless you and keep you safe.

May the Lord cause His face to shine upon you, and be gracious and compassionate towards you.

May the Lord bestow His radiant countenance upon you, and give you everlasting peace.

Numbers 6:24-26 APTA

the wisdom that is from above is first pure, then PEACEABLE, gentle, and easy to be intreated, full of mercy and good fruits, without partiality, and without hypocrisy.

James 3:17 KJV

Ye shall go out with joy, and be led forth with peace

Isaiah 55:12a KJV

Therefore being justified by faith have peace with God through our Jesus Christ Romans 5:1 KJV

Let the peace of God rule in your hearts. To this peace you are also called to be a part of one body. Let's be thankful.

Colossians 3:15a ARA

MAY MERCY BE UPON YOU,
AND PEACE, QUIETNESS
AND LOVE BE ABUNDANTLY
MULTIPLIED. JUDE 2 ARIA

HOW BEAUTIFUL ON THE MOUNTAINS ARE THE FEET OF MESSENGERS WHO ARE BRINGING GOOD NEWS, WHO ARE ANNOUNCING PEACE, WHO ARE BRINGING GOOD NEWS OF GOOD, WHO ARE ANNOUNCING SALVATION; SAYING TO ZION, "IT'S YOUR GOD THAT REIGNS!"

ISAIAH 52:7 ARIA

His name shall be called WONDERFUL, COUNSELLOR, THE MIGHTY GOD, THE EVERLASTING FATHER, THE PRINCE OF PEACE. Of the increase of his government and PEACE there shall be no end.

Isaiah 9:6-7a KJV

The fruit of righteousness is sown in peace

of them that make peace.

James 3:18 KJV

The accomplishment of
righteousness will be peace,
and the outworking of
righteousness is quietness,
assurance and trust forever.
My people will settle
in peaceful homes,
in safe dwellings,
and in quiet resting places.
Isaiah 32: 17-18 ARIA

May the Lord of Peace Himself give you Peace at all times, and by all means in every way. The Lord be with you all.

2 Thessalonians 3:16 KJV

THEREFORE BEING
JUSTIFIED BY FAITH,
WE HAVE PEACE WITH
GOD THROUGH OUR
LORD JESUS CHRIST
ROMANS 5:1 KJV

The God of
peace be with
you all.
Amen.

Romans 15:33 KJV

Shalom

A Prayer for Peace

Thank you Heavenly Father for Your peace that You
give to us that comforts and surpasses understanding.

Thank you for giving us Your Word, the Bible, to hold onto in
times of trouble. That we can hope in You to protect us when
seasons of life seem dark, and yet Your peace remains with us.
Thank you for Your promises of restoration and that You welcome
us into Your wonderful healing light.

We pray that Your Word will continue to enlighten
and encourage us about Your love and peace that
You have for Your precious children.

Thank you Lord, that You are our ultimate Saviour,
who rescues us during hard times, and brings
comfort, joy and peace to our hearts.

Amen.

PEACE WALL SCRIPTURE ART

First published in 2021

by Dawnlight Publishing

This edition published in 2024

ISBN 978-1-99-117699-8 (hardcover)

ISBN 978-1-99-117683-7 (paperback)

Peace Wall artwork designed by Mike Burrows Graphics.

Book layout and illustrations by Mary Marinan.

Text, artwork and creative book concept copyright © Dawnlight Publishing 2024.

Scripture quotations from the King James Version and American Standard Version ~ public domain use.

Scrippture quotations from the Artistic Revived and Inspired Adaptation (paraphrase) ~ copyright © 2023 by Dawnlight Publishing. Used by permission. All rights reserved.

A catalogue record for this book is available from the National Library of New Zealand

All rights reserved. No part of this publication may be reproduced, stored in a retrieval system, or transmitted, in any form or by any means, electronic, mechanical, photocopying, recording or otherwise, without the prior written permission of the publisher. The only exception is brief quotations for the purpose of printed reviews.

Scripture Art Books

Scripture art coffee-table style
hardcover books

Smaller
paperback size

Companion Writeable
Scripture Art editions
with writing space to
add your own prayers
and verses

Other titles by Dawnlight Publishing

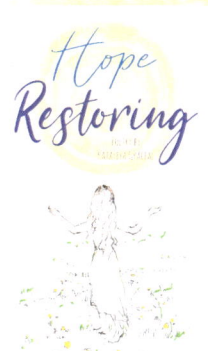

Books, and books and journals in-one

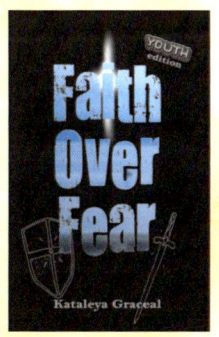

Poetry

www.ingramcontent.com/pod-product-compliance
Lightning Source LLC
Chambersburg PA
CBRC090833120626
46547CB00009B/676